Soccer
Captain

Soccer Captain

MICHAEL HARDCASTLE

Orion
Children's Books

First published in Great Britain in 1994
by Orion Children's Books
a division of the Orion Publishing Group Ltd
Orion House
5 Upper St Martin's Lane
London WC2H 9EA

*A catalogue record for this book is available
from the British Library*

Typeset by Deltatype Ltd, Ellesmere Port, Cheshire
Printed in Great Britain by
Clays Ltd, St Ives plc

ISBN 1 85881 060 4

Contents

1

Missing
the coach

CALLUM COULDN'T STOP THINKING about football and the fate of his team. All the time he and Ricky had been at the Leisure Pool his worries about Hurlford Hawks had been floating to the surface. Frowning, he snapped at the waistband of his scarlet swimming trunks and looked hard at Ricky.

'So, what's going to happen now, do you suppose?' he asked.

'Oh, you'll get chucked out because you're not allowed to sit here without any clothes on. We've all read the Leisure Pool rules. And I'll get kicked out, too, just 'cos I'm with you!'

Callum's irritation showed. 'I'm not talking about this place. I mean our heroic Sunday League team. What's going to happen if Sandy really has left us for good?'

'Oh, he's gone, that's definite,' Ricky declared. 'He said he'd had enough of us and, who knows, we might even improve when we're left on our own. That's just how he said it. Oh, and he also said if he ever worked as hard for another team as he's worked for us then he hopes the players will really appreciate him. In other words, he hopes they won't be like us.'

Callum's brown eyes narrowed. 'That just means he's hoping for a leaving present. Well, I'm not making a contribution. I mean, what's Sandy *really* done for us? Just let us sink to the depths of the League, that's what. My dog's got more sense of direction than Sandy Sanderson. Tramp always pulls in the same direction – forward! With Sandy you never knew whether you were supposed to be exploring the left wing or the right wing or even going backwards! What sort of coach is that?'

'Let's just forget him,' Ricky advised. 'We've got to think about ourselves now, how we're going to cope without someone to fix our travel and tell us what the opposition's like. I mean, it's too late in the season now to pack up and play for another team, isn't it? The Kellington League doesn't allow transfers after teams have played several matches.'

Callum's big left toe was now scratching hard at his right calf as if he were suffering a severe itch. In fact, he was trying to work out what to say because until a few moments ago he'd idly been wondering which team he could sign for if Hurlford Hawks broke up following their coach's departure. He'd fancied the idea of joining Drumblade Cutters, one of the Hawks' rivals. Callum Douglas Collins (often called Disco by team-mates because of his first two initials) was sure that the Cutters would be delighted to have the services of a wandering winger-cum-midfielder with terrific ball skills and an instinct for scoring unexpected goals. That, anyway, was how he saw himself in his more down-to-earth moments. What a pity, he reflected, that his family had no plans to move house to another town so that he could start afresh with another team. He didn't doubt that Ricky Dezille knew what he was talking about so far as League regulations were concerned. So Callum would have to play with the Hawks after all, provided, of course, the rest of the team stayed together.

'Do you think we should *advertise* for a new coach?' he suggested. 'You know, put a card on the supermarket noticeboard? Doesn't cost anything to customers, all part of the Asda service, they say. My mum found a buyer for her old pram that way. In twenty-four hours, too. She was dead pleased.'

Ricky was shaking his head. 'Don't think that'd work. People wouldn't search a noticeboard for teams to join. No, I reckon we'll have to get help from one of our dads. Any ideas?'

Callum raised an eyebrow. 'You've just mentioned one, haven't you? Why not yours? I mean, you know mine's not at home these days.'

Ricky had half-turned away, as if to study the goings-on in the fun pool. It was a moment or two before he spoke at all. 'Well, mine's not at home these days, either. Well, not much. Mum's, er, told him not to bother coming back unless he, er, changes his ways.' He turned back, adding defiantly: 'So he's no good to us.'

Callum just nodded his head as if he were only hearing something he'd expected. 'Oh, well, we'll think of something,' he said philosophically. 'If everything else fails, I suppose Mum might help by giving us lifts to matches. She's actually thinking of getting a bigger car for herself now she can't drive Dad's. So –'

But before he could explain further, a man wearing a lemon T-shirt and green tracksuit trousers clamped a hand on his shoulder, the strength of the grip causing Callum's brown eyes to open wide. 'What do you think you're doing, son? I've seen you in here before so you must know the rules about not lazing around here in your swimming gear. Right?'

Callum reacted swiftly. 'Sorry. Honestly, I was just heading back to the pool. It won't happen again. Can I go back in the water? *Please?*'

His politeness paid off. The attendant suddenly smiled, ruffled Callum's floppy brown hair and then pushed him towards the pool. 'You've had your final warning,' he reminded him. 'I'll not be so kind next time.'

'Power,' Callum muttered to Ricky as he reached the foot of the steps leading to the tube slide called The Black Bomber. 'Power is all these guys think about. They just need *somebody* to boss about. Just my luck it was me today.'

He raced up the sixty or more steps to the fearsome and frantic tube he couldn't resist, though it still half frightened him to death as he went into the first vertical drop. You hadn't a clue where you were going because the slide was pitch black. Apart from the screams of anyone else who might be shooting through it, the only sound to be heard was the gurgling of the water itself.

He emerged like a bullet from a gun, plunging into the pool in the midst of a waterfall and only narrowly missing a casual swimmer floating on her back. She shouldn't have been there and Callum told her so, though perfectly politely. He was usually careful in his dealings with the opposite sex whatever their age; it was men he would curse and try to outwit. Then he went under water for as long as he could manage, tweaking a couple of passing legs while he had the chance and enjoying the astonished reactions of his targets. Callum had travelled through the torture tube so fast – and yet it had seemed like a long journey. For the moment, however, he could't bring himself to try the entire trip with his arms rigid by his sides. That would require courage of a higher order than even he possessed at present.

Ricky sauntered along the side of the pool. He admired Disco's nerve and willingness to take wild risks, something he himself was too timid to try. So far he'd managed only the Yellow Tube, known as The Twister, and that was tough enough for him. There'd been moments when he was certain he was going to drown as water frothed over him. Ricky felt much more confident on the soccer pitch, even when he had to dive at an attacker's feet to prevent a certain goal. At least he could usually see what he was doing and where he was going. In the tubes he was powerless to control his own destiny.

'Come on, Disco, it's time we weren't here!' he yelled.

Callum heard the call but didn't respond; he knew very well that his time was up and that if they didn't hurry they'd be late for the team meeting. Then he spotted the attendant in the yellow T-shirt. The guy was pointedly looking at his watch and then frowning in Callum's direction. He lingered no longer. Hastily scrambling out of the pool he raced to the changing-rooms where, moments later, Ricky caught up with him.

'What a twist!' Callum exclaimed, slapping his chest and thighs with his towel. 'I had to come out just when the current was going to be turned on. Then I could've gone round and round for ten minutes. That's always terrific.'

'Listen, we've got to get moving,' said Ricky. 'The rest of the squad will probably go home when Sandy doesn't turn up and you and I aren't there, either. I bet you Davey Ramsden is the first to disappear. You know how miserable he gets if anything goes wrong. Lack of staying power, that's always his problem. Sometimes it must be an effort for him just to get through a normal match!'

Callum was pulling on his socks first, a ritual he'd begun on reading that was how a famous international player always dressed before a match because he felt it was lucky for him. He shared Ricky's view but he wasn't going to hurry. If Sandy had deserted them it wouldn't be long before the Hawks had to pack up. So his mind was still dwelling on how he'd go about getting himself into another team. One possibility was to try a league in a neighbouring town. That would overcome the complication of his registration with Kellington Sunday League. The chief problem, though, might be to persuade his mum to transport him to matches so far from home every week of the season.

'Cal, come on!' Ricky pleaded. 'I'll go on my own if you don't speed up.'

Callum grinned and yanked on his pants. 'Don't panic, we'll have loads of time when we get there to sort things out. If nobody turns up, well, that'll be it. Our future will be no future at all.'

They left the changing-room and went to collect their cycles from the sophisticated new lockers at the foot of a ramp close to the entrance to the Fun Centre. Their meetings always took place at The Hut on the edge of a wooded area beside a complex of playing pitches. It was truly a multi-purpose building for in the course of a week it might be occupied by practising bandsmen, a barber-shop quartet, scouts, trainee trampolinists and country dancers.

Mid-evening on Mondays was not, for some reason, a popular time with any other organisation, and Mr Sanderson had secured it for their weekly get-together. It was hardly an ideal time to start training for the next match but he pointed out that it enabled him to analyse their Sunday performances before the players had forgotten them. Although mostly constructed of wood, and fairly isolated from other buildings, The Hut never suffered from vandalism, probably because of its popularity with so many local people of all ages.

Despite Ricky's insistence that they would be late, he and Callum arrived a few minutes ahead of the official meeting time. The only other player there was Joe Kelly, predictably bouncing a yellow tennis ball on his instep as part of a routine of ball skills he rehearsed whenever he wasn't doing anything else.

Since being appointed captain a few matches ago, stocky, dark-eyed Joe had changed his attitude to his team-mates and become quite bossy. Yet, because he wasn't much of a player himself, he wasn't really respected by them. All too often, they had to try to make up for his mistakes in defence. Callum's theory was that

Joe had been appointed skipper simply because he could be relied upon to do whatever Sandy ordered him to do. Joe never had a bright idea of his own that could be tried out.

'When's Sandy getting here?' Joe snapped the moment he saw them.

Callum shrugged. 'From what I hear, he won't be turning up at all. Not tonight and never again.' He was rather pleased with the sound of that phrase and so he smiled at Joe genially.

'You're joking,' Joe said, but without conviction. He'd heard rumours that Sandy was up to something and he was worried. For a start, his own position as skipper would be in jeopardy if someone else took over. Worse, he might be dropped from the team altogether. In his heart, Joe knew he wasn't anywhere near as good as he liked to make out. But he felt he was getting better all the time and his incessant training with a small ball, an idea he'd read about in a magazine, was, he felt, bound to improve his skills.

'He's joking, isn't he?' Joe now appealed to Ricky.

'No, he's not,' Ricky confirmed. 'You know that Red's dad was at the match yesterday? Right, well, Sandy told him he was giving up, asked him if he fancied the job himself now he was taking an interest in the team. But Red's dad said no way, he just wanted to enjoy watching football. Sandy said he didn't think there *was* enjoyment in our games any more. We just weren't good enough to entertain anybody. Well, that's what Red told me and Disco. If Red turns up tonight, you can ask him yourself, Joe.'

'But if he's giving up he should have told *me* first,' Joe complained. 'I mean, I *am* the captain of this team. It's just not fair to tell others first.'

'Oh sure, you're the captain,' Callum agreed with a rather twisted grin. 'But that won't mean anything if there isn't a team to lead, will it?'

Joe missed his kick completely in his private training routine and the ball ran away into a corner of the hut. He didn't go after it and his face paled as he took in the implications of Callum's remark. 'It won't be as bad as that, will it, if Sandy backs out?' he asked waveringly.

'Well, you're not a good organiser, are you?' said Ricky. 'I mean, Sandy's always done everything in that line himself. So I don't think there's much hope. The Hawks will have been shot down, we'll be as dead as that old dodo!'

Callum couldn't help laughing at that bit of imagery although he would instantly have agreed with anyone who pointed out that the fate of their team wasn't a laughing matter. In any case, he believed they would be saved somehow, just as he was sure that his dad would come home again for good one day.

'Oh, what's so funny? Have we signed the next England centre-forward – or has Joe been kissed by a girl?'

The newcomer with the highly-developed sense of humour was Hanif, who had a joke for almost every occasion. He was one of the Hawks' most successful players, a midfielder always willing to fetch and carry the ball in any situation and a positive ferret in the way he'd dive into a scrum of players to secure possession.

'Listen, this isn't funny at all, it's dead serious,' Joe told him, ignoring the crack about a kiss, a reference to Joe's recent careless remark that he'd rather give a defence-splitting pass to a team-mate than get a kiss from the most glamorous film star in the world.

'Tell me before I have a fatal heart attack,' Hanif implored him, hands crossed theatrically over his chest.

Joe did so and Hanif listened without making a single interruption, humorous or otherwise. To the bright-eyed Hanif the future of the team was of compelling importance. Even though the Hawks were low in the League table and didn't appear likely to win anything this season, his own ambitions were unchanged. His intention was to play for England one day.

Selectors for youth and county and other representative teams might turn up at any match at any time, either casually or to run the rule over a particular player they'd seen before or had recommended to them. But, of course, they'd also note anyone else playing outstandingly and his name, too, would enter their notebooks. Hanif was determined to make sure that, if ever a selector turned up at a Hawks match, he would be the player to catch the eye, his would be the name scribbled in the book.

The tale of woe had to be repeated as other players drifted in during the next few minutes. Every time the door opened they all hoped it would be Sandy who walked in – and each time the hopes were dashed. Even though no one really liked him, they all recognised that a team without a coach would soon be a team in trouble.

'Come on,' said Joe, trying to rouse himself as well as the rest of the squad, 'let's get on with *some* training. Let's go and have a kick around if nothing else. You never know, Sandy may just have been held up. Could be along any minute.'

By now nobody believed that but they responded to the skipper's suggestion because it made sense. They hadn't taken the trouble to come to The Hut just to slink home again without so much as kicking a ball.

Joe's hand was literally stretching out for the handle when the door swung open. A tall, attractive woman with shoulder-length fair hair and wearing a lilac-and-white tracksuit strode in. Her smile was as warm and friendly as her first words.

'Hi, you must be the Hawks,' she greeted them. 'I'm really glad to meet you. My name's Lynda Hesketh and I hear you need a new coach. Well, I'm really keen to take on that job, to help you all make the most of your talents. I believe I can do you a lot of good. And I'm sure we'll all get along famously.'

2

Lynda
takes over

CALLUM WAS THE FIRST TO RECOVER from the shock of that announcement. He hadn't any idea of how she had heard about them but he sensed she meant what she said.

'Are you good at football, then?' he asked. It was, as it turned out, the best question he could have asked, far better than inquiring about her coaching skills.

'Well, yes, I think I am,' she replied, her smile so wide they could see how white her teeth were – like a film star's, Hanif would have said, if anyone had invited a description. 'You see, I play regularly for Kellington Ladies and have some coaching experience with them – oh, and an office team before that.'

'What position d'you play?' Hanif immediately wanted to know.

'In midfield mostly but sometimes up-front – a bit

like you, actually, Hanif,' she replied, and they all took in every word she uttered.

Hanif's mouth was open in astonishment. 'How – how do you know my name?'

The strength of her smile didn't diminish for a second. 'Well, I've watched you play, as it happens. And I've heard my brother use your name when he was coaching.' She paused momentarily and then added: 'That's what I've come to explain about, you see. My brother is Bobby Sanderson, or Sandy as I think you all call him, though perhaps not to his face.'

Questions were forming rapidly but it was Hanif who got in first. 'Did he send you to us? I mean, has he asked you to take his place and be our official coach?'

'No, definitely not, Hanif,' was the response. 'It's my idea, my idea entirely, although Bobby has no objection to it. I can tell you all, I'd really like to take over, if, that is, you want me. But, of course, it's up to you. I'm offering my services and you have to decide whether you want them. Simple as that, really – or, just possibly, difficult as that.'

Joe decided to ask the next question because so far he hadn't said a word and, as he never had to remind himself, he was Hurlford Hawks' captain. 'Have you got a car and will you drive us to matches? Oh, and did you know I'm the team captain?'

By now the smile had weakened and was replaced by a serious expression. Lynda Hesketh knew this wasn't a moment to look as though she were laughing at Joe's proud declaration. 'Yes, Joe, I know my brother gave you the captaincy when Dean left – when was that, five, six, matches ago? Yes, I thought so. Oh yes, and the other very important matter: I certainly do have a car, a family-size car, and so I'll be able to take those players to games who wouldn't otherwise have a lift. It'll give me a chance to talk things over on journeys. Useful, that.'

'Oh, great,' Joe responded enthusiastically. He wasn't going to make any other comment until it suddenly occurred to him that, as captain, he ought to speak for everyone. 'We'll be glad if you'll be our coach, then, Miss.'

'Ah,' she said quickly, 'better not call me Miss like that. Makes me sound like a school teacher and I'm not that, I can promise you. If you do want me to be your coach, all of you, well then, I think you'd better call me Coach or Boss, if you prefer that. That's sensible, isn't it?'

Nobody questioned that, but there was something Callum felt it was vital to know. 'Why did Sandy– your brother, I mean – pack up being our coach? He hasn't really told anybody that, only *hinted* to a few people, like Red's father.'

Red Herring, who'd been listening intently to everything that was said, without wishing to contribute, now nodded vigorously. He approved of Callum. In his view he was easily the best player Hawks possessed. He would never admit it but he tried to emulate Callum's style wherever he played in the side. Sandy had used him as both central midfielder and striker at various times.

'Good question,' Lynda agreed. 'Well, it's not that he's just got fed up with you or anything like that. But, to be truthful, he's had an approach from another team to take them over – a team of much older players. I think he's flattered that they've asked him. It's not unusual, you know, for coaches and managers to move to other teams in different leagues. Happens all the time, doesn't it? Players swap teams as well when they get the chance and, well, Sandy was ready for a new challenge.'

She guessed that some of the boys were probably wondering why Sandy hadn't told them this himself. Sandy had admitted to her that he didn't think the Hawks had much future as a team, that he felt he'd taken them as far as he could in the League. But, of course, it would be hurtful to them all to tell them that. She'd told him he was being unfair and he admitted it; and it was then she realised that *someone* in their family owed the boys a better deal. And because football was becoming a passion with her she decided to take his place, if the Hawks would accept her. On that score, she had great doubts which might take a long time to be eliminated.

'So Sandy – Mr Sanderson, I mean – he's not moving to another team in our division, then?' Callum persisted, determined to know the extent of what he now regarded as their ex-coach's treachery.

Lynda Hesketh shook her head vigorously, which set her hair dancing. 'Definitely not. As I said, his new team is much older than you. Some of the players have already left college and have got jobs. You're Callum, aren't you?'

He nodded, not surprised that she knew his name. Sandy made a habit of shouting it during matches when he felt Callum wasn't doing what he should be doing. Callum had grown used to being a focus for instructions and responded only when he agreed with them.

'Right, any other questions?' she asked briskly, making sure she looked at everyone as she glanced round the dressing-room, aware that their expressions varied between the eager and the wary. 'I know it's better to get some things sorted out first but I also expect it'll be easier to deal with most matters as we get to know each other better. Okay: I must ask a question of you, *all* of you. Is there anybody, at this moment, who *doesn't* want me to be your coach? Don't be afraid of speaking up. Honesty is very important in all relationships and if anyone has serious doubts about working with me, it's best to say so now.'

She guessed that if anyone raised an objection it would be Callum or, possibly, the pale boy with russet-coloured hair who she didn't know by name but thought might be Red Herring. She was right, but the boy with the appropriate name remained silent as the rest.

'Well, that's fine, thank you,' she resumed at her usual brisk rate. 'Just one other thing and then we'll get down to some serious ball work which is what I'm here for. I'm going to be frank because it's silly to be anything else. I expect that some of you will be worried by the fact that I'm a woman and I'll be in a boys' dressing-room. At your age you're bound to be self-conscious about sexual differences, I know I was when *I* was your age. But that's *not* going to be allowed to make any difference to any of us. Before long, you'll get used to the fact that I'm close to you here as well as during matches. I have a son of my own, just about your age, so there isn't anything I haven't seen before. Remember this: embarrassment is for those who are silly and immature. I want you to be as natural in the changing-rooms as you are on the pitch. And I'll be the same. Okay?'

Some faces had already taken on a slightly pink hue

but, to her relief, no one looked really embarrassed or on the verge of giggles. In some ways, she knew, groups of boys were easier to deal with than groups of girls. No doubt there'd be moments to come when one or other of them would test her out with their own versions of being frank but she was confident she'd be able to meet such challenges.

Just one question was asked, by a boy she hadn't really noticed so far and whose name she promptly asked. It wasn't a question she could have anticipated. 'I'm Davey Ramsden,' he told her. 'You said you had a son, our age. Well, will you be putting him in our team? You know, giving him the place of one of us.'

The bright smile was back. 'Definitely not, Davey. Marcus, my son, already plays for another team. It wouldn't be fair at all to try to take him away from his own team and fit him into the Hawks. In any case, he might not fancy the idea of taking *more* orders from his mum!'

'Oh, good,' Davey said, spontaneously, to the amusement of some of his team-mates. Most of them could guess why he'd asked that question: he was perhaps the poorest player in the side and one that their former coach had picked on relentlessly when things were going wrong for the team, as they had done frequently this season.

'Now, we haven't a lot of time this evening before the light goes altogether so we can't get much done. I need to see you all in action in a proper game before I can work out what is needed to lift us up the League. However, every team, in my view, can improve on its ball skills, so that's where we'll begin. Callum, here are the keys to my car, the red VW estate round the back.

Inside you'll find some flagposts, short ones, old corner flags, actually. Oh, and a couple of footballs. Could you fetch them, please?'

3

Training
to win

CALLUM WAS SURPRISED SHE'D chosen him to be her errand boy but he didn't object; he was quite keen to see what sort of car she drove. But it occurred to him as he collected the gear that she must have been confident they'd accept her as coach, otherwise she'd hardly have brought football equipment with her. Plainly she was well organised: but would she be any good at *managing* a team in a cut-throat junior Sunday League? Did she really know enough about the game to devise new tactics for different matches and outwit the opposition? Callum hoped so. Hanif wasn't the only ambitious player in the Hawks.

The moment she had her hands on the flagposts, Lynda Hesketh stuck them in the ground on the training pitch in two parallel lines about two metres apart and then, with minimal delay, she divided the players into two teams. She made no attempt to choose one boy ahead of another for any reason but simply split them into equal numbers.

'This is called a slalom relay because it's a bit like that weaving in-and-out race on skis,' she explained. 'The teams start level and each player has to dribble in-and-out between the flags and turn at the end to repeat the run on the way back. Then he passes to the next player. The idea is to finish ahead of the other team, naturally, but if anyone misses out a flag for any reason he's got to go back and do that flag again. So close control is needed. It's more important than speed. If you can't *control* the ball in your possession then you're not going to be much use to your team, whether doing this slalom or playing in a real match. Ball control comes first in football. Remember that.'

Hanif nodded fiercely. 'That is true, Coach. All top managers say a lot about controlling the ball at all times.'

'Thank you, Hanif,' said a gratified Lynda, though she hoped he wasn't the type to agree publicly with everything she said. Over-enthusiastic support could be almost as difficult to cope with as its opposite, sullen silence.

'So, when are we going to start this game?' Red inquired, politely but firmly. He had lined up directly behind Callum and was eager to show off his skills.

'Right now! On the word "GO" the first player in each team sets off and *must* complete the course properly before passing the ball to the next man over the starting line. You can cheer on your friends as loudly as you like. I always like a good atmosphere in training. Okay . . . GO!'

Callum touched the ball away instantly but didn't allow it to run too far ahead of him as he swerved neatly to his left round the first flag. His concentration was total and so he wasn't aware that he was the one the Hawks' new coach was really studying. Joe had claimed the right to be first in the other team but even before he came to the second flag he had to run back to retrieve the ball. His problem was that he was using only one foot to dribble with, his right. Consequently he was making a hash of his attempts to take the ball to the right.

'Hurry up, Joe, hurry up!' Hanif, the next player in his team, yelled. 'We're miles behind them. Hurry up!'

By now Callum's team was cheering him on passionately and Ricky was jumping up and down in his excitement and hollering: 'Go, Disco, go, go, go!'

Lynda was delighted with the boys' immediate response to the very first training exercise she'd set them. They couldn't have demonstrated more enthusiasm even if she'd offered rewards for the winning team, something she was totally opposed to; in her eyes, the ultimate success of the team brought its own rewards. At the back of her mind, though, was the worry that perhaps they'd appeared to accept her too easily; probably most of them would just wait to see how the relationship developed before making their feelings known.

Joe was getting into a worse state as a result of Hanif's shouting and Lynda decided to step in.

'Hanif, I think that's enough. Joe's doing his best even if he's not doing very well.' Then, realising what she'd said she hastily added: 'It's not as easy as it looks.'

Callum was making it look quite easy, however, and was slipping the ball crisply to Red before Joe managed to turn at the end of his line of flags. Hanif was in despair, but managing to restrain himself from further shouts.

'The other team started before I did,' Joe blustered when at last he completed the course. 'You ought to've stopped 'em, Miss, pulled 'em back and made 'em go again.' Lynda didn't know how many of the other players had heard Joe or would take any notice, but he had to be dealt with because 'whingers', as she thought of players like Joe, would go on for ever if not pulled up immediately.

'Joe, that's not true. I was watching the start very carefully and you went off simultaneously. In any case, I'm the referee in this game and players have to learn never to argue with the ref. Understand?'

This time Joe just nodded, too unhappy with everything that was happening to him to speak.

Hardly anyone else was paying any attention to this exchange, for the excitement was building up again. Although Callum and Red performed skilfully and established a good lead over Joe's side, matters were evening up because of Hanif's brilliance. Like Callum, he could use both feet and his fleetness of foot in midfield situations now stood him in excellent stead. He caught up much of the lost ground and Ricky was showing unexpected skills to improve their position still further. As a goalie, Ricky had few chances to try out his ball skills. But he'd played as a winger for his previous team until losing his place through injury and being unable to win it back. The only vacancy had been in goal and since then no one had allowed him to play anywhere else.

But that flourish by the round-faced goalie was the 'B'

team's last moment of success, for Davey Ramsden, the last player on Callum's side, finished well ahead of his opposite number and was cheered mightily by his team-mates. Davey, unused to personal applause, started jumping up and down on the spot for the sheer joy of hearing it.

'Well done, boys, well done!' Lynda enthused. 'You played that in just the right spirit. Most of you did, anyway! Did you enjoy it?'

Because the rest chorused 'Yes!' Joe didn't feel he could say 'No,' but that was his reaction. What he really objected to was the unfairness of the game: in his view the posts should have been placed further apart so that he could have coped more eaily when using just one foot to control the ball. He knew from experience, though, that the rest of the squad rarely agreed with him over anything.

'Good!' Mrs Hesketh continued. 'Because if you really enjoy a training session then it must be doing you good and you're bound to be getting something out of it in terms of improving skills. Right, I think we've just time to try out one more exercise. This one tests the other major skill you need in addition to ball control – passing the ball. Passing it quickly and accurately.'

'But what about shooting?' Red inquired forcefully. 'I mean, if you can't *hit* a ball strongly enough to beat a goalie you might just as well pack up.'

His new coach didn't reject that view out of hand as her brother might have done if someone disagreed with him or offered up an alternative suggestion. 'What do you think about that, Callum? And you, Joe?'

Joe, still quietly seething with resentment and disappointment, didn't hesitate. 'Yeah, Red's right.

You've *really* got to be able to bash a ball and you need strength for that. That's why I eat the proper food to build up muscles.'

Lynda blinked. That was a comment she could never have predicted. Glancing at the others, she detected what might have been smirks but nobody laughed at Joe's announcement about his choice of food. But then, she reflected, boys always respected sheer strength and toughness.

'Callum?' she invited again, not least because she couldn't even begin to guess what he was thinking.

'Well, I think passing is very important,' he said in a deliberate manner, nodding slowly as he spoke. 'If you don't get the right sort of pass when you need it you've no chance of going anywhere, have you? Like taking on the defence in the box or beating a defender for speed on the wing. Yeah, I agree.'

Nobody argued with that point of view, either, and Lynda sensed that, with a couple of exceptions, the Hawks preferred to let others express their opinions rather than volunteer their own.

'Okay, well this is what's going to happen,' she went on briskly again. 'I'm putting you in threes and this exercise is a bit like pig-in-the-middle. Two players have to try to pass the ball to one another and the one standing between them has to try to intercept it. Passes have got to be made with just the *right* foot first – the left is for standing on! Then we'll switch and you use only the left. This can be tiring so we wouldn't keep it up for long even if the light was better.'

One or two of the players indicated they didn't understand what was expected of them so Lynda decided a demonstration was needed. She chose Hanif,

Joe and Red, with Hanif as the player in the role of interceptor. Using one half of the pitch only, the three were allocated zones of equal size measuring roughly eight by eight in metres and each was told he had to keep to his own area.

'Off you go, Joe, just send the ball with your right foot to Red, trying to avoid Hanif,' she repeated. 'When Red gets it, he'll pass it back the same way. But if Hanif gets possession three times he's won the game and you two have lost! Okay? It's really simple, so let's get going.'

It was simple, too simple for Hanif, as it turned out. The moment the ball was on the move he was after it, anticipating how and where it would travel. But then, Joe wasn't showing much method in trying to get the ball across to his partner, much to Red's dismay. Once Joe tried to push the ball across a vacant space with his left foot and immediately two of his team-mates yelled: 'You can't do that! It's right foot only.'

Naturally, Lynda was pleased with such a reaction and so she quickly organised the rest of the players into trios. Watching Joe lumbering about she sighed; she should have known he hadn't a hope of outwitting anyone as nimble and alert as Hanif.

'Right, that'll do,' she ordered, striding forward to collect the ball from a beaming Hanif. 'Let's try it the other way round with Joe going into the middle and you now using your left foot.'

'But that's not fair!' Joe protested predictably. 'Hanif's a lot faster than me – us. I'm a defender, he's a midfielder. So –'

'Joe, in soccer *everybody's* got to be fast these days,' she told him. 'Full-backs need to be as speedy as wingers. That's what I want for the Hawks. Lots of pace and ball control. An exercise like this is aimed at sharpening up reflexes and speed of thought and movement in *everyone*.'

'And it does, it's great, Miss,' Hanif exclaimed, his face glowing with delight as well as his exertions.

How, Lynda wondered, was she going to stop them calling her Miss? She'd have to think of something.

She wandered round the various games, offering a word of advice here, praise there, but sharp criticism nowhere for she regretted being harsh with Joe. Perhaps he was used to it, though again, probably not, as her brother Bobby had appointed him team captain. For the life of her she couldn't see why he'd done that unless it was to boost Joe's confidence, which could well be low most of the time.

The energy of the players surprised her. For many of them it had probably been a long day with a variety of experiences at school and home and perhaps elsewhere, too. Boys of this age often appeared to have endless zip and stamina – and then, all of a sudden they flopped, went down like a deflated balloon. She had seen it with her own son who, until he was really exhausted, wouldn't admit to feeling even a little tired.

Fiercely, she blew her whistle, which reminded her again that she must be careful not to make anything seem like a school activity or ritual. But she wasn't going to try bellowing to get attention. 'Well done, boys, well done. You worked really hard there and I hope you enjoyed it. But that's quite enough for one night. Don't want you getting home and being told by Mums or Dads you've worn yourself out at football. Now, before we part, anyone got any questions?'

But most of the faces before her were simply blank. Even if they had questions it was not the time to ask them. They needed to go home. Yet Lynda herself also needed to know that they truly wanted her to be their leader.

'All right, there'll be another time to talk things over,' she said quietly. 'I know you're playing Blackness Park on Sunday and I'll be there for that, of course. But I'll get a message to all of you before then, telling you about my – *our* – plans. I'll also be having a word with some of you later in the week. Now, if anyone needs a lift, I've plenty of room in my car. So, just say . . .'

Most of them simply melted away into the night without a further word to her or to anyone who wasn't a close friend. Lynda stretched out a hand to detain Callum and then Hanif. 'Before you go, boys, can I ask a favour of you?'

'What's that?' Callum asked warily, whereas Hanif nodded vigorously, his eyes still full of life.

'I know this is a lot to ask,' she said, 'but I'd be really grateful if you'd do some quiet thinking about the team, *our* team, the Hawks and then write a report for me on what you think our strengths and weaknesses are. Be absolutely honest, say just what you think. Don't worry about, well, criticising a friend or even yourself! Just write the truth as you see it. Will you do that?'

Hanif was already nodding his head again but Callum remained cautious. 'What d'you want them for, if we do them?'

'They'll be a huge help to me in getting to know the team and how you play, Callum. I want to make up my own mind about the Hawks, not just ask my brother what he thinks. In any case, I've a good idea of his views on your strengths and weaknesses! As I told you, I haven't seen you play often enough to make a proper judgement. That's why your ideas will be a good guide to me. There's no sinister reason behind my request. And if you don't fancy the task, well, just say so, I won't be offended. I'm only interested in building the best future I can for our team.'

'I'll do it, Miss,' Hanif gushed. 'I'll do it. D'you want it tomorrow? I can –'

'No, Hanif, definitely not! I don't want you to rush this thing, just the opposite. I want your *considered* thoughts, your deepest feelings about the Hawks. Work out first what you really believe about the team before you write a word. If you can let me have your views when we meet on Sunday that'll be fine. Oh, and Hanif, *please*, no more Miss! Okay?'

'Yes, Mi– er, Coach! Sorry!'

She turned to Callum, who was rubbing a thumb under his jawbone as if still trying to come to a decision. 'Cal, it really doesn't matter if you don't want to, so just forget –'

'No,' he cut in sharply. 'I'll do it. But you might not like it if I say what I really think.'

The smile was back as she thanked him. 'The truth, that's all I want, Callum. So don't bother about *my* feelings. Right, then, we'd better all get home. I'll be in touch – and I'll see you on Sunday.'

'Why don't you want to do this report, Disco?' asked Hanif when they were on their own.

Callum shrugged. 'Not quite sure, except that it makes me think I'm going to be a sort of spy, reporting on the enemy, or something like that. Makes me wonder what she's up to. It's a bit worrying.'

Hanif nodded, slowly this time. 'Yes, see what you mean, Dis. Hadn't thought of it like that. Yes, I agree with you, it *is* a bit worrying. But I'm still going to do it. I think she needs our help, you see. She's going to do all she can for us. So she's got to have somebody on her side.'

4

Blackness
black-out

IN THE DRESSING-ROOM JOE KELLY, pacing rapidly from one end to the other and back again, was beginning to get desperate. Most of the rest of the Hawks looked less concerned and Ricky Dezille was actually quite philosophical.

'Quit worrying, Joe, she'll turn up, I'll bet on it,' he remarked. 'She told us she'd be here and kick-off isn't for another ten minutes yet. Bags of time.'

'Probably her car's broken down in traffic or there's been a family crisis like the baby choking on its food,' Hanif offered. 'That's what happens in our family.'

'Lynda Hesketh hasn't got a baby, just one son our age called Marcus,' Joe shot back, unable to take comfort from anything but the arrival of Hurlford's new coach. 'I'll bet she's packed up already. She'll have listened to Sandy telling her we're rubbish with no future.'

'No, she won't,' Callum insisted. 'I talked to her last night and she's dead keen to see us win today. She said she feels she's going to bring us luck.'

The captain frowned. 'She didn't talk to *me* last night. So why –'

'Look, Joe, she talked to everybody this week, right?' Callum cut him off. His gaze swept the dressing-room and everyone else nodded. 'She just thought I might need a lift today, so that's why she phoned me up. Oh yeah, and she also wanted my opinion on something. So –'

'What about?' Joe couldn't resist asking.

'Oh, whether our defence was really any good and whether our skipper might score any own goals today!' Callum supplied on the spur of the moment. There were times when Joe Kelly's glumness and suspicions got him down. Callum's comment was plainly a joke and some of the players laughed aloud.

'That's not funny, Collins!' Joe protested. 'I do my best for this team, all the time. I'm the best tackler. That's why I'm the captain, why Sandy chose me and nobody else. I've only once scored an own goal, and that was a complete fluke. It happened –'

But nobody was listening to him because their new coach had arrived. Most of the boys instinctively got to their feet to greet her, several in relief that she had turned up and, therefore, must believe in them as a team. Joe fell silent but looked as pleased as anyone.

'Sorry I'm late, boys,' she greeted them beamingly. 'Just one of those things. There was a change of plan and I had to go and see somebody in a hurry. Sort of family mini-crisis, if you like.'

Hanif shot a glance at Callum and mouthed: 'Told you so.' Callum grinned.

'Anyway, I can't do much now but tell you to go out there and do your best,' Lynda went on. 'Remember to control the ball and pass intelligently. We'll have a tactical talk at half-time. But I'll send out instructions if anything needs changing urgently. So, Joe, keep an eye on the bench when you can. Okay, everybody?'

Some murmured 'Yes', others nodded and only Joe started to ask a question. But at that moment the referee poked his head round the door and said, quite sharply: 'You boys should be on the pitch by now. Wake up!'

Guiltily, they raced out but, again, Lynda managed to detain Callum and Hanif. 'Have you got those reports?' she asked. 'I could have a quick look at them during the first half if I get a chance.'

Without comment, they both turned back, rummaged in their sports bags and produced scribbled sheets. To Callum it felt just like handing in homework to a teacher who would discuss it with him later; but he didn't say that. He didn't say anything.

Callum's thoughts now were on how he was going to play against a team with a rising reputation for attacking play and ruthless defence. He had no fear of being hurt by aggressive, stronger players and he was perfectly prepared to torment them with his skills if he got the chance.

'Come on The Park!' a man whose face was as red as it was round was shouting even while his team was warming up in the goalmouth kick-in. Blackness didn't look as though they needed any encouragement. There was a fierce urgency about them and their red-and-black striped shirts with black shorts somehow seemed appropriate colours. In contrast, the Hawks, in their much milder blue-and-white stripes with pale blue shorts, suddenly looked rather tame to Callum Collins. Perhaps they needed early vocal support, too.

Joe Kelly, however, usually said nothing at all to anyone unless a player made a mistake. Occasionally he clapped his hands but Callum thought that was really to help motivate himself rather than his team-mates. Joe won the toss and rather grandly indicated that the Hawks would kick-off rather than choose which end to defend. It flitted through Callum's mind that their coach may have suggested this tactic to their skipper but Callum couldn't see any advantage in it. Indeed, there was a slight slope from one goalmouth to the other and the Hawks were now facing it. Wouldn't it have been better to play downhill in the first half, so putting early pressure on the opposition?

Aaron Quaintance, Hurlford's main striker, pushed the ball sideways to Callum when the whistle sounded and Callum automatically transferred it to Hanif. The midfielder cleverly changed direction to evade an on-rushing tackler and then hit an accurate floating pass to Aaron, now cruising through the middle.

Aaron, dark-eyed and stocky, had few real ball skills but his persistent, bustling manner could upset some defences. This time, however, the Hawks' striker wasn't sharp enough to take the pass and bring the ball under control. The Blackness central defender gathered it with ease, made smooth progress for several metres and then delivered a splendid cross-field pass to his left-winger.

'Come on The Park!' roared the florid-faced supporter even before the ball reached its target. He was aware that everyone around the pitch, and probably those a hundred metres away in any direction, would hear him. It was his belief that the more noise he made the better his team would play. Sometimes he was right.

The long-legged winger jinked sideways the moment he was in possession and then, challenged by Joe, pulled the ball in the opposite direction and attempted to accelerate. Joe went after him and made a desperate tackle. Somehow the winger kept his feet in spite of a stumble and might have made further progress but for the referee's whistle.

'That was on the rough side,' the official told Joe, wagging a finger warningly. 'Better not do that again if you want to avoid a booking. I see you're the skipper, too.'

Joe scowled but retreated for the free kick he'd conceded. Blackness pushed extra players up immediately and it was plain they were going to make the most of this early opening. It was the central defender who took the kick, the one who'd earlier supplied his winger with a perfect pass; and, to the surprise of Hurlford's defence, he did it again, hitting the ball once more towards the flank rather than into the penalty area. It looked like a ploy that had been tried successfully before: and it worked again.

Again the slender wingman took possession, calmly making sure he had a clear route to goal before increasing his pace. Red Herring was the first to try to close him down but when the winger swerved past him with effortless ease, Red didn't try to chase him. Instead, he relied on Joe to make amends for that earlier crude tackle.

But Joe was being cautious this time, determined not to be made a fool of by this confident opponent. So instead of going in at him, he back-pedalled, back-pedalled at increasing speed as the Park player, cheered on by their loudest supporter, attacked relentlessly. 'Get him, get him!' Red yelled at his skipper but Joe was taking orders from no one. He was sure he was doing the right thing in waiting for the perfect moment to pounce. In any case, he was expecting the thin boy to pass to a team-mate or switch the ball sideways to the edge of the box for someone else to have a shot at goal.

The winger jinked once more, appeared about to dart forward, half turned sideways and then, with a shot of astonishing force, hammered the ball, right-footed, into the top of the net. Ricky had every right to be as amazed as anyone but he was the one who had to move. He didn't.

'Goal!' the scorer yelled as, arms aloft, he wheeled away. 'Goal! Great start, Park!' yelled the florid one. 'Great, great, GREAT!' chortled the Blackness captain, racing across to embrace his new hero, and the scoring winger was so pleased with life he even allowed himself to be kissed.

Joe sank to his knees. He couldn't help himself. His team was a goal down within a minute of the start of the match and, in his heart, he knew he should have done more to try to prevent it. But who would have guessed that the long-legged boy in the red-and-black shirt possessed a *right* foot with such power in it?

Callum shrugged, turning to Hanif to exchange expressions of utter dismay. Because his attention had been diverted by the antics of some Park supporters he hadn't seen the immediate build-up to the goal but the sight of the roof of the net rising was enough to depress him. Instinctively, he glanced across at Lynda Hesketh, who'd taken up a position just over the halfway line in the Hawks' half of the pitch.

Mrs Hesketh was shaking her head gently and Callum sympathised. What a way to start with a new team as their coach! He wondered if she would signal to indicate she wanted changes in defence, as Sandy would've done. But she didn't.

'We've had it now, I expect we'll let in half-a-hundred goals,' Davey Ramsden muttered to Joe as they lined up for the re-start. Davey had been sent into so many different positions under Sandy's leadership that he sometimes found himself wondering what he was supposed to be doing. At present he was a defender and therefore one of those responsible for the success of Park's first attack.

'Never expected him to score from *that* distance,' Joe said for the umpteenth time since the goal was scored. As soon as he got off his knees he started offering excuses to anyone who'd listen. He, too, had cast glances at his coach but it seemed to Joe that she was deliberately ignoring him. He thought the least she could have done was offer some useful advice on how to contain Blackness' lethal attack. It was surely obvious to everyone that he, Joe, couldn't do *everything* on his own.

Blackness surged back into the Hawks' half almost immediately, Hanif having been bundled off the ball in such brutal fashion he was staggered that Hurlford weren't awarded a free kick. Once again the ball was switched to the talented flying winger. Joe inevitably was still cautious about attempting a proper tackle but he didn't want to keep backing off, either. Luckily for him, he didn't have to do either for, in a crafty change of direction, the winger veered to the touchline before turning to hit a long cross with his left foot. His target was Park's towering centre-forward, Minton, but the ball eluded him and fell neatly for his co-striker to try a snap shot. Though he hit the ball well enough, the shot lacked power and Ricky was thankful he could take it easily in his arms in front of his chest. The attackers were too well trained to try and hustle a goalie already in possession of the ball.

By bouncing the ball up and down several times, both to demonstrate his confidence and to give his team a breather, Ricky drew the ire of the ref who signalled furiously to him to get on with the game. Ricky gulped, bounced the ball nervously once more and then tried to punt it down the pitch. But he miskicked badly, the ball sliced away to hit poor Davey on the back from where it rebounded to a startled but alert Minton. And the Blackness centre-forward was not a player to miss a glittering open goal. Tapping the ball ahead of him for just a couple of paces, and without a Hawk within metres of him, he took careful aim and let fly.

With Ricky still bemused by his dreadful error and thus helpless to stop it with a hand or any other part of his body, the ball flew into the back of the net to put Blackness two-up in less than three minutes of the kick-off.

This time Hurlford's new coach did have something to say. 'Get a grip, you Hawks! What are you thinking of?'

It wasn't a comment she was proud of, it wasn't even grammatical, but she was impelled to let her team know she was there. She knew they'd be in a state of shock but that was no reason to keep silent. Plainly they needed someone to take charge and help them recover.

'Hanif,' she called urgently, 'Stick to their big centre-forward, don't let him have another kick. He's the one they're going to play to. Put him in handcuffs – or leg-irons, rather!'

'But I'm half his size!' Hanif protested. 'I'll not be able to –'

'Just keep snapping at his heels, Hanif,' Lynda instructed. 'Big dogs hate little dogs getting in their way, I promise you.' She knew it wasn't a particularly elegant or appealing image but Hanif didn't object, he simply nodded his understanding.

Then, to her surprise, Lynda saw the ref hurrying towards her. 'I don't allow coaching from the touchline during a match,' he said, scowling. 'You know the rules, don't you? If it happens again, I shan't hesitate to ban you from the touchline altogether. So you have now been given an official warning.'

Rather as Ricky had done a few minutes earlier, Lynda gulped. The truth was she didn't know the rules of the Kellington Sunday League but she was well aware that touchline coaching wasn't permitted anywhere, officially. Most coaches managed it discreetly and most referees turned a blind eye to the offence. Today's official obviously was a stickler for every rule in the book. It didn't worry her that the Hawks must be aware she'd been reprimanded by the ref; very probably it impressed them that she was willing to tangle with him. Perhaps now they *would* get a firm grip on their game. She began to work out what to say to them at half-time.

'I'm defending now,' Hanif informed Joe as he dropped back.

'Well, we need help against this lot,' Joe muttered predictably. 'They're dynamite. I thought that winger was bad enough but the centre-forward, well, he's a load of trouble.'

No one had said a word to Ricky who was wishing he played a different game from soccer. He'd been hoping the new coach would permit him to switch roles and become an outfield player, possibly on the right wing where he could turn his dreams of being a goal-scorer into reality. But after his terrible clearance had resulted in a gift for Blackness he'd very likely be dropped from the team altogether. Even Joe hadn't shouted at him; but then, Joe had problems of his own.

Callum, who'd hardly touched the ball so far, insisted on a return pass from Red, now in midfield in place of Hanif. Slowly, but displaying real determination to keep possession, Callum jogged down the left flank, almost taunting opponents to come at him. He knew that if the Hawks didn't hit back quickly Blackness Park might easily over-run them. The confidence of the Park players meant that they allowed Callum to keep moving forward; after all, he couldn't threaten their fortress from that distance and none of the other Hawks was in a position to take a pass that might spell danger. They'd all heard that Hurlford didn't possess much talent, and the past few minutes seemed to have confirmed that. So now they all believed Park could attack at will and probably score at regular intervals.

With no hint of what he had in mind, Callum suddenly surged forward, swerved one way, went in the opposite direction and then very neatly nutmegged an opponent by slipping the ball between his legs and collecting it before the red-and-black-shirted player could turn round. The red-faced Park supporter was silenced by such skill and moments later was open-mouthed with admiration as Callum exchanged a one-two with Red, who'd sensibly raced up to give support, and then calmly chipped the ball over the head of the next rival who tried to confront him. Callum himself could hardly believe that every trick he attempted was coming off. At this rate he might be able to slice through the entire opposition and put the ball into the net without hindrance.

Quickly, and quite cleverly, Park resorted to the only certain way of stopping Callum's progress. Two of their toughest defenders closed on him simultaneously and ruthlessly scythed him to the ground without so much as a glance at the ball. Callum grazed his knee but wasn't otherwise hurt. He didn't need to ask for the referee's backing.

The official imperiously summoned both offenders to him and unhesitatingly put their names in his book before issuing the sternest of warnings. The free kick he awarded was only a metre or so from the edge of the penalty area.

'Well done, Callum, well done!' his coach sang out as the hero of the moment hobbled away. He wasn't really hurt at all but he thought it did no harm to let the ref and opponents believe that he was incapacitated, even if only temporarily. It just might work to his advantage in the next few minutes. He would have liked to take the kick himself but knew he couldn't get away with that *and* pretend he was unfit. Instead, he told Davey Ramsden under his breath: 'Hit it as hard as you can over to Red. Nobody's watching him.'

As usual, Davey was willing to do exactly what he was told and he couldn't have struck the ball better. Because Minton, Park's towering striker, hadn't bothered to drop back to assist his defence, their lack of height was a distinct disadvantage on this occasion. The ball flashed across to Red who instinctively pivoted and let fly a tremendous shot on the volley. Unfortunately, his aim was at fault and the ball sailed harmlessly high over the bar.

'Good effort, Hawks, keep attacking!' Lynda sang out, only for the florid one to guffaw again, just as he'd done when the shot was plainly off-target.

'Sorry,' Red signalled to Davey, who really didn't mind a bit. He was simply pleased that *his* free kick had created such a chance for his team-mate, just as he was delighted to have been given the task and to have struck the ball so well.

Inevitably, Blackness retaliated immediately, swinging the ball from wing to wing before finding Minton with a high pass on the edge of the box. He was smart enough to nod the ball down to a team-mate before accepting a quick return and darting to a shooting position.

Joe's attempt at a tackle was again misjudged but this time Ricky was on hand to clear up. Throwing himself at Minton's feet as the striker took one step too many, he smothered the ball – and all danger. He had every reason to look pleased with himself as he got to his feet, bounced the ball firmly only a couple of times and then punted it towards the halfway line. The coach let him know she was impressed as she clapped loudly and put thumbs up in his honour.

With Callum sticking to his 'temporarily disabled' plan the ball wasn't pushed out to him when Hurlford had possession; on the other hand, no one was giving it away cheaply and Park were having to work harder for any success. However, with a two-goal lead they could afford to be patient. They kept probing for weaknesses like a dentist searching for cavities in a patient's teeth, but the Hawks were beginning to look more solid at the back. Ricky, although still yearning to play up-field, handled confidently everything that came his way and, somehow, was managing to cope with the crises that involved him. So, when the ref blew for half-time, the Hawks could feel that the first half perhaps hadn't been a total disaster for them after all.

5

Going forward

'YOU DID WELL, REALLY WELL,' their coach greeted them as they returned to the changing-room, which caused one or two to blink. It was definitely not what Sandy would have said in identical circumstances. 'You made a bad start but you fought back and that's the spirit we need.'

'But the forwards haven't been getting forward, have they?' Joe remarked boldly, taking advantage of Lynda's benevolent attitude to his own error. 'So if we don't score goals we can't win, can we?'

'Hey, come off it, Joe!' Red protested instantly. 'You're the one who messed things up by giving them their first goal. If you'd –'

'Okay, okay,' Lynda cut in hastily. 'We're not going to get anywhere by throwing blame around, Red. Joe knows he made an error, so does Ricky, but the important thing is the *team* is getting better all round. That's the plus side of life at the moment.'

Red turned away to hide his muttered oaths. Why hadn't she criticised Joe? After all, he'd made the first remark about who wasn't doing the right thing. Red was one of the brightest members of the team and he'd noted that at present no one was arguing with their new coach. So he'd wait for a better opportunity to say publicly what he thought of her.

'How's your ankle, Cal?' she inquired now. 'It was your ankle you hurt, wasn't it? Want me to have a look at it?'

He shook his head. 'No thanks. It's not so bad now. I'll, er, do more running in the second half.'

'Good. I think you and Red can combine well if you are both a bit more positive in going forward. I also like the idea of you, Davey, coming up from the back to join in attacks. You've got speed, so we must make use of it.'

Davey glowed. It was wonderful to get some praise from a coach.

'But what about me?' Hanif inquired anxiously. 'I mean, Miss, *I* should be up in the attack when possible. But I'm stuck at the back with the defence. I think I'm wasted there, Miss.'

She sighed, very loudly. 'NOT Miss, Hanif. I'm telling everyone that for the last time! Just get it into your head that I'm your *coach*.' She paused, saw that Hanif looked mortified and gave him her most dazzling smile. 'Hanif, you're doing a great job at the back, just what we need. You've helped to shore things up.'

She could see that Joe didn't like that remark at all but it couldn't be helped. Fortunately, he didn't challenge it and, for the next few minutes, they all relaxed and sucked on the oranges she'd provided. Before they went out for the second half, she made a couple of tactical changes: Callum to move infield more, Alan Roimond, a midfielder, to play like a sweeper. 'Fight for every ball,' she told them. 'Go all out to win. You can do it, Hawks!'

As he went out, determined to prove he was the best player on the pitch, it occurred to Callum that Mrs Hesketh hadn't said a word about the report she'd asked him for and he was sure she couldn't have read it yet. Had it all been a waste of time? He hoped not because he realised he quite liked her. Undoubtedly she knew more about football than any of them had suspected when she'd introduced herself.

Blackness, disappointed by their failure to add to their lead before the interval, charged into attack from the kick-off and once again the brilliant left-winger led the way.

'Go on, Alan, close him down!' ordered Joe. 'Get at him, go on!'

Alan, however, hesitated, uncertain what to do. 'But I'm supposed to stay back, pick up anybody who gets right into our penalty area,' he revealed.

Joe frowned. 'Who told you that?' he inquired in the manner of someone who doesn't believe a word of what he's just heard.

'Lynda, of course!'

This time Joe blinked. 'So when did she tell you that? I never heard her say a thing to you.'

Alan shrugged. 'Well, she did, just before we came back on the pitch. I think you must have been in the loo.'

Now Joe chewed the inside of his lip, trying to decide

what to do next. 'I'm the skipper,' he declared a moment or two later. 'So you do what *I* want.'

By the time Alan decided to obey his captain's orders it was too late: Blackness had increased their lead through the winger's sorcery and their tall centre-forward's speed of thought.

Outwitting both challengers, the winger suddenly lofted the ball into the middle instead of cutting across the open space in front of him. Unmarked now by Alan and too tall to be foiled by Hanif, Minton cleverly chested the ball down, turned into the box and fired a shot into the roof of the net before Ricky could even guess where the ball might go. It was an opportunist's goal, scored with almost nonchalant ease.

'Easy, Park, EASY!' their bellowing supporter saluted them.

Callum, glancing quickly at the touchline, saw that their coach had covered her eyes, doubtless with exasperation after what she'd told them at half-time.

Joe didn't speak for the next fifteen minutes, by which time Park had failed to increase their lead, because of resolute defending by some of his team-mates. Hurlford themselves managed a couple of attacks when first Callum and then Aaron made solo runs that simply petered out through lack of support. By then, Park knew the points for this match were safely in their keeping.

With almost the last kick of the match Callum had his first shot at goal. With Park relaxing their grip a little, Aaron steamrollered up the middle, brushing aside a couple of distinctly physical challenges that the ref for once ignored. Callum crossed behind his team-mate to run a parallel course on the right. 'Yours, Dis!' Aaron suddenly yelled and hit a strong pass ahead of him. Aaron was hoping for a return but Callum took the ball in his stride, knocked it past a full-back who moved slowly because he'd hardly been in the game, and took aim. He knew he was really too far out for a shot but he hoped he might take the goalie by surprise. After all, the goalie, too, had been seriously under-employed in this game.

The shot was on target, still rising towards the roof of the net, but the fair-haired boy between the posts was just as alert as when he'd taken a shower that morning. Taking the ball in both hands above his head he snuffed out Hurlford's one remaining hope of finishing the game on a high note.

'It could have been worse, I suppose, but we have a lot to talk about, a lot to work on,' Mrs Hesketh greeted her players as they trudged back into the changing-room. 'Now I've seen you in action I have clearer ideas about what's necessary. We're not going to have an inquest now. You look a bit tired, to say the least, and I want you to be mentally bright when we discuss plans. I'll just say this and then leave you to have showers, get changed and go home. Don't despair, you'll soon get better. When we've sorted a few things out I'm absolutely positive the Hawks will start climbing the League. Who knows, you might even start *flying*!'

Nobody actually laughed but there were a few wan smiles. Most had expected to be on the receiving end of a battery of rockets.

'But I do want to have a word with you two,' she murmured, moving across to Callum and Hanif whose clothes were on adjacent pegs. 'So, when you're ready, I'll be in my car. Okay?'

They nodded, guessing she wanted to analyse their views on Hurlford's strengths and weaknesses. Then she made her way over to Joe, took him on one side and talked for a few moments. They couldn't prevent themselves watching and so saw his expression change and gloom take over. He didn't once glance towards them so they could assume they weren't being mentioned.

'She's taking the captaincy off him, I'll bet anything,' Hanif whispered fiercely to Callum. 'So who'd you think she'll choose now? I hope it's me! I'd be really good at it.'

6

Changes all round

THERE WAS PLENTY OF ROOM FOR both of them to stretch out on the back seat of the coach's estate car but they sat at either end, unable to relax. Lynda had turned to face them, one arm resting on the back of the front passenger seat, the other on the steering wheel.

'I've read your reports, boys, and I'm grateful that you took the time and trouble to do them,' she said crisply. 'I completely accept what you say, Callum, about the Hawks having no plan or, if there was one, that my brother changed it weekly. He is a bit like that so I can appreciate your shrewdness in working it out. I also agree with you, Hanif, that everybody needs to put a bit more effort into their play, and play as a team, not as a bunch of individuals. We saw that happening today and it's got to be eliminated. Players have got to work for each other, *talk* to one another, call out when necessary about covering a gap or going for an opening. So thanks for all your help, you two.'

She paused and Callum wondered what was coming next. Because of Hanif's forecast it wasn't a surprise. 'I've told Joe Kelly that he's not going to be captain any longer. I really don't think he's ever going to be any good at that job. I don't need to go into the reasons because I'm sure you're aware of his limitations.'

They didn't say anything, simply waited for her to break the news of who *was* to be captain. Hanif's nails were practically piercing his palms but he didn't feel the pain.

'Cal,' she went on in a brisker tone, 'I want you to captain the team from now on.'

There was a kind of strangled gasp from Hanif while Callum was so astonished he searched for a lurking smile on her face. It wasn't there. She was perfectly serious.

'But why me?' he asked. 'Why are you dropping Joe?'

'Joe lacks confidence in himself, so he can't inspire confidence in others. He worries about the smallest detail and that gets in the way of thinking about the game as a whole. He has no tactical sense, or, at least, he's never displayed any. I could go on, but I won't. It wouldn't be fair on Joe.'

'He's very loyal,' Callum pointed out. 'He'd die for the team. He'll probably die if he's dropped. He'll not get over it.'

Lynda had to be cautious about what she said next. 'I didn't say I was going to drop him. If he's playing well and really contributing to the team he'll stay in the side.

But he might need a break to get over the disappointment he's bound to feel at no longer being captain. If he desperately wants to play for the Hawks, as you say, then he'll fight his way back. He'll *force* me to pick him again. And you, Cal, will know how to encourage him, how to give him a lift. Won't you?'

He shrugged. 'I'm not sure. I just like playing for myself really. I like making things happen and –'

'Exactly!' she cut in. 'Of course you do. But not only for yourself, you do it for the whole team.'

'Mrs Hesketh, why not me as captain?' Hanif demanded, believing he still had a chance while Callum appeared to be making up his mind.

Her radiant smile returned. 'Hanif, you're *vital* to the team – all your energy and determination. But, in a way, you're *too* involved because you're so keen all the time. I don't want you to stop playing like that, and I'm sure you would if you had to think about tactics and what's best for others. You're our midfield dynamo. But I do want you to be vice-captain, ready to take over if Callum is hurt or missing for any reason. Provided, of course, that he's willing to be skipper.'

Callum was chewing the inside of his lip, bothered by thoughts of the responsibilities of the job. Did he really want them? He knew he could be enthusiastic about almost anything he did, so if he became skipper he'd have to give lots of energy to that, too. 'Maybe the rest of the squad won't want me as captain,' he pointed out. 'I don't get on with all of them, don't even *like* some of them.'

'That's natural,' she replied. 'It'd be impossible to get on with everybody you meet or work with or share a sport with. Cal, they respect you, that's the important element. They respect your skills – and your attitude.'

Hanif nodded but didn't say anything. Callum was shaking his head, so she asked what was troubling him. 'I've been told my attitude isn't always right. I agree. I once just walked off the pitch, walked out of a game. Sandy was mad at me for that.'

She frowned. This was news to her. 'So what happened?'

'Oh, there was this lad on the other team, kept trying to kick my kneecap off, or any other bit of me he could hit. I could never get him back because he ran off so fast. Did it to other players, too, but I was his main target. Just an assassin, that's what he was. I asked the ref to do something about it but he ordered me to get on with the game, made out he'd seen nothing. Sandy wouldn't complain, either, when I told him at half-time. He should have *noticed* what was going on but he didn't want to know. So in the second half I walked off in protest. The ref still didn't say anything but Sandy was furious. Banned me for three matches, told me I'd be lucky to get a game with the Hawks again. Said I was disloyal. So . . .'

'What about the other players, your team-mates?' Lynda glanced at Hanif, but he remained silent. His set expression told her nothing at all.

Callum shrugged. 'Oh, some said I did the right thing, others said I'd let the team down. But we didn't lose the game, we drew.'

'Any other examples of your attitudes, Cal?'

He thought for a few moments and then admitted: 'Well, I don't like obeying some of those stupid little rules at places like the Leisure Centre. You know, where you have to wear shoes or a shirt in certain areas, just to fit in with everybody else. I often break those sort of rules just because, well, to *show* they're stupid.'

Lynda nodded and said: 'But, really, you do approve of rules, you *are* law-abiding. That's how you were when that opponent was kicking you. He was infringing the rules and you appealed to authority, the ref, Sandy, to uphold them. They let you down. So you made your protest in a sensible way. I mean, you didn't try to break the same rules by kicking him, did you?'

Callum grinned. 'I might've done if I could've caught him!'

'But you didn't, so that doesn't apply. We'll look to the future, not the past. That's why I don't refer to Sandy's time when he was coaching the Hawks. That's history.'

Callum laughed. 'He wouldn't have picked me as captain, that's dead certain. Once he said that the only reason I wasn't a complete "one-off" was because I like wearing our blue-and-white shirt!'

'There you are then!' Lynda exclaimed triumphantly. 'Sandy was recognising your loyalty and I've already said that's something I prize highly among players. It's one of the reasons why you and Hanif will be such a good pairing to lead the side.'

She turned the beam of her smile on Hanif but his face was still expressionless and she knew he was trying to come to terms with his disappointment. But she was confident he'd respond to Callum's brand of captaincy.

'But what will you want me to do that's different from just being a player?' Callum inquired.

'Take control on the pitch, be my voice, if you like. Wear my authority as well as the captain's armband. Cal, you'll see things happening it'll be impossible for me to see, such as whether someone's feigning injury or pulling out of tackle or not competing for a fifty-fifty ball. That sort of thing. You'll have my authority to take the necessary action to put things right. I also believe you'll lead by example. So, will you do it – do it for me – do it for Hurlford Hawks?'

He didn't answer immediately and Lynda realised she had no idea what he'd say; she wasn't even certain how she'd react if he turned the captaincy down. Would she offer it to Hanif? All she could be sure of was that Hanif'd accept it like a shot.

'Okay, then, I'll do it,' Callum announced after an interval, to her great relief.

'Wonderful!' she rejoiced, holding out her hand as if she were congratulating another adult. Callum, however, solemnly shook hands with her and, to the surprise of all of them, Hanif, too, exchanged hand-shakes with his new skipper. In that moment, Lynda knew she'd made the right choice with both boys.

'Well, that's the perfect note to finish our talk on,' she added. 'I'd like to tell you about my ideas for future games, about how we plan for different opponents, but that's just not possible yet. I've not had a chance to see them in action and work things out. But there's time for that.'

'So we'll just take each match as it comes, right?' grinned Callum, quoting the ordinary football manager's favourite phrase.

'You could say that, more or less,' she agreed. 'But at least this way we'll be ourselves. So we'll let other teams worry about *us*.'

7

Before the crisis

UNDER THEIR NEW LEADER, Hurlford Hawks made an impressive start. All the horrors of the Blackness Park fiasco were swiftly forgotten as they tore into Burridale in their next match. Many teams had vowed to 'dig a grave' for the ill-named Burridale but not many managed to do it. On this occasion, however, the Hawks' whirlwind start to the game at home had Burridale shivering with fear of what might follow.

In the week following his appointment, Callum was readily accepted by the rest of the players as their new captain; predictably, Joe Kelly resented the change but only Red Herring was prepared to listen to Joe's grumbling. Hanif had decided he didn't at all mind being vice-captain for, as he pointed out to friends elsewhere, he was now 'only a heart-beat away from the captaincy.' He told his mother that, too, and when she replied that it was a macabre attitude he explained: 'But that's what they always say about a Vice-President of the United States of America!'

They'd also fully accepted Mrs Hesketh as their coach, apart from Red, who kept muttering that 'women shouldn't be in charge of *our* game – it's a *boys'* game.' However, she had dropped him to substitute for the first game of Callum's captaincy, so other players gave Red a sympathetic hearing while advising him to fight for his place whenever he got on to the pitch. It was becoming clear that she preferred to play Alan Roimond in midfield. Round-faced and blond-haired, he could be as sulky as Red when he felt like it, but his promotion boosted his confidence. Alan, who liked gadgets of all kinds and was forever trying to invent a new one, began telling everyone that their female coach was the best invention since the can-opener (which wasn't a comparison Lynda herself would have cared for had she heard it).

Callum's attitude didn't change immediately he put on the captain's armband. In fact, he appeared almost to be testing Lynda's view of him when next she entered the changing-room before the Burridale match. His habit of wandering around the room wearing only his socks before changing into his playing kit was rather more than a superstition these days. He wasn't going to alter his routine just because of her presence and the other players waited to see her reaction. But all that happened was that she gave her new skipper a frank, appraising glance, smiled as warmly as usual and turned away to talk to someone else. Callum didn't really know what he'd expected her to say or do but he supposed this low-key response was typical of her.

On the pitch Callum took the business of tossing-up seriously and told his opposite number that the Hawks would kick-off rather than choose the end to defend. Lynda had said they should attack from the outset, really put their own stamp on the match and show the opposition they were in for a torrid time. Joe, remembering his days as captain, frowned from the touchline where he was stationed as substitute.

Hanif, who'd been told to resume his midfield role and forget about man-to-man marking, eagerly joined in the opening attack, determined to impress his coach with his all-round contribution to the game. It was in his mind that if anything happened to Callum, such as an injury or illness or drastic loss of form, then he, Hanif, would at last take over the captaincy. Aaron Quaintance went over on a typical bustling run towards the right flank while Davey Ramsden's eyes gleamed at the prospect of participating in an early attack. His job, Lynda had told him, was to move forward as an overlapping full-back whenever the opportunity arose. Full-backs, she explained, should not be mere defenders: they must always be regarded as vital support raiders. Davey, thrilled to be allotted his own specialist's role, was intent on making the most of his chance of a permanent place in the team. He'd played against Burridale in the past and knew that their defence was unreliable. So this was his opportunity to make a lasting impression on Hurlford's brilliant new coach, as Davey regarded her.

'There's got to be good running *off* the ball as well as on it,' she emphasised at their previous training session.

And she had displayed a great deal of tactical awareness in planning some of the moves she wanted them to try out. 'We don't want anybody hanging about, simply wondering what's going on and what to do next. We've got to PLAN for what we WANT to happen. That's the way the professionals do it, and that's the way we're going to do it.'

'It amazes me she hasn't brought a blackboard and some chalk with her,' Red Herring had muttered to Joe at that point. Joe nodded his agreement but wasn't prepared to voice his real opinion in front of her.

Now, in the opening moments of the game against Burridale, Lynda Hesketh's shrewd planning paid off. The Hawks knew what was expected of them and set about achieving those objectives. Callum's change of direction on the edge of the penalty area fooled one defender and caused another to stumble at a crucial moment. Aaron, seeing his chance, swooped on the ball like his aerial namesake, took it on a couple of metres and then, with splendid timing, pushed it in front of the in-rushing Hanif, who thus had a clear view of goal.

It should have put the home side one-up, for Hanif had only the goalkeeper to beat. In his haste to get on the scoresheet, however, poor Hanif hit his shot straight at his opponent who somehow managed to cling on to the ball in spite of his surprise at getting even a touch of it. Hanif was mortified, hanging his head like a repentant criminal as he turned away. He simply daren't look at Lynda who was sadly shaking her head.

'Next time, give me the ball,' Alan urged Aaron as they waited for the outcome of the goal-kick. Alan was as keen as anyone to make a good impression, for his father was the one parent who'd turned up to watch the Hawks.

Normally, Mr Roimond, who lived on his own after his divorce, wasn't much interested in soccer but when his son couldn't stop talking about his team's new coach he decided he ought to see what she was like. Mrs Hesketh was a great deal more attractive than he could have imagined and it wasn't long before he was wondering whether she was divorced, too. So that she couldn't fail to be aware of his loyalties he shouted: 'Well done, The Blues! You nearly had 'em there. Keep it up!'

Nobody had ever called the Hawks 'The Blues' before, but Callum and his team couldn't doubt that he meant them, for Burridale were in all-red. Five minutes later he really had something to shout about when Hanif unselfishly released the ball after cutting into the area for Callum to take it in his stride and sidefoot it past the stricken keeper. The Hawks had scored their first goal under their new management. Mr Roimond's only disappointment was that it wasn't Alan who'd put the ball in the net, but he was pleased to see how happy the new 'Blues' were making the slim, fair-haired coach.

Joe hadn't made the mistake of not joining in the applause, but he could work out that if the Hawks won this game without him then it would be doubly hard to get back into the team.

Callum shrugged off congratulations with the battle cry, 'One goal's not enough,' a phrase his coach would treasure and repeat regularly thereafter. He agreed with her that a captain should lead by example and that's what he intended to do at all times. So he made a point of thanking Hanif for the vital pass and then urging his defence to be ready to repel the inevitable counter-attacks. Lynda, listening on the side-lines, nodded approvingly. She didn't doubt she'd made the right choice as captain.

Burridale had neither the strength nor determination to fight back and ten minutes later a dreadful blunder in the goalmouth presented Aaron with the chance to toe-poke the ball over the line for the Hawks' second goal. After that, the game was never a contest and Hurlford won, easing up, by four clear goals. It could have been more.

'Every goal counts in the final analysis,' their coach reminded them in the changing-room before realising she must sound like the accountant she was at other times. 'At the end of the season, goal difference could be vital if we're level on points with another team and promotion is at stake. So if you squander goal chances as you did in the second half than you may have to pay for them later.'

She knew it was probably unrealistic to mention promotion but it would do no harm to encourage ambition among the squad, most of whom, like Davey Ramsden, were inclined to be pessimistic much of the time. On the other hand, their experiences while Sandy was their coach hadn't helped them to view life in any other light. When they started to undress and head for the showers she told them they'd discuss future plans at the next training session, congratulated them again on their victory, and left. It wouldn't have bothered most of the boys if she'd stayed but one or two were still embarrassed by the fact that their coach was female. Before long, she hoped, they'd get over such trifling worries.

8

*Countdown
to a crisis*

THE HAWKS WON THEIR NEXT MATCH, too, although not as convincingly. Before they turned out against the Rope and Anchor's junior team, the Cadets, Mrs Hesketh did a bit of fine-tuning in the 'engine room – midfield', as she put it. Hanif was to play wider on the right, with Alan Roimond adopting a more central role; Alan had shown in training that he was one of the fiercest tacklers in the squad and she wanted him as their ball-winner. He relished the practice session so much after being told this that he left two of his team-mates nursing bruises. Once again his father turned up for the match and drifted towards Lynda to strike up a conversation. She was perfectly polite to him but made it plain she wasn't willing to be distracted from her job of watching and encouraging her players. 'If you lose concentration then you'll miss something that's really important and the team suffers,' she pointed out. Mr Roimond nodded his understanding but his disappointment was obvious as he retreated a little way along the touchline.

The pub team had a band of supporters with them and they cheered lustily when Ricky Dezille was tested in the opening moments of the game by a powerful shot from the Cadets' fast centre-forward. Ricky, however, fielded the ball fairly nonchalantly and then set up the Hawks' own attack by throwing the ball to Davey for him to make a long run down the flank. During training sessions there was no keener member of the squad than Ricky, though it was his footwork that mattered to him, not his handling. He was certain he'd be a brilliant winger or raiding full-back and so he still dreamed about giving up the gloves for glory on the wing. The best thing was that Mrs Hesketh understood that, sympathised with his ambitions, and had promised that if she found a goalkeeper good enough to replace him then he could have his chance as an outfield player. Ricky was starting to idolize the Hawks' new coach.

Joe Kelly was still stuck on the sidelines as a substitute and his gloom was deepening. In the previous match Lynda, not wanting to interfere with a winning team, hadn't brought on a substitute at any stage. Joe concluded that she wouldn't do it in this match, either, and so he'd remain in the cold. Nobody seemed to care that only a couple of weeks ago he had been the Hawks' skipper. So, if he wasn't going to get back into the team, he might as well pack the game up. He wasn't going to waste his time mooching up and down the touchline. It wasn't in Joe's nature to try to bounce back after a setback.

The Cadets' early fire was dampened down by Hurlford's first goal which arrived in the twelfth minute. Once again, Callum made the initial break-through, taking the ball cleverly in the pit of his stomach from a badly hit pass by Alan. When it dropped to his feet Callum calmly steered it past an opponent whose wild swing was more like a haymaking swipe than an attempt at a serious tackle.

Looking up, Callum saw that Davey was winging down the flank, eager to contribute. Callum sent him the ball to run on to and then, if he had the skill, swing over a centre. Davey didn't manage quite as well as he'd hoped but the ball defeated the defence anyway and Aaron was on hand to slam it into the net while the goalkeeper made up his mind whether to stay on his line or dive forward. Lynda, applauding the goal, was really congratulating Callum on his perception as well as the quality of his pass. Davey, of course, was thrilled to have done so well and he and Aaron embraced with fervour.

Two minutes later the ball was in the net again but this time it was all down to luck, good as well as bad. From a mêlée in the middle of the Cadets' half, a defender, trying to hack the ball clear, succeeded only in hitting it against a team-mate; from him it rebounded into no-man's-land between that group of players and the goalkeeper. Because the ball came off an opponent, Aaron was on-side as he darted to gain possession. This time the goalie swooped to save, actually got a hand to the ball but wasn't able to prevent it bouncing upwards and over his outstretched body. And the spin on the ball took it remorselessly into the yawning net.

After that, the Hawks tended to relax, though Lynda

kept signalling that more effort was needed. At half-time she translated the signals into strong words that some were able to swallow and others couldn't. Davey and Red, for instance, were beginning to believe that a magic formula had been found to bring the Hawks unending success. Even when Rope and Anchor pulled a goal back early in the second-half, Davey and Red remained confident their team would win again. Which they did by that narrow margin of 2–1.

Lynda debated whether to make changes for the next match against Reskington Raiders and thought it might be time to restore Joe to the side.

However, when she consulted Callum on the telephone the night before the game he remarked it was surely wise never to change a winning team; Sandy, he pointed out, was always 'chopping and changing whether we won or not and I think that messed us up.' Lynda took that comment seriously for she was still determined to let the Hawks see that her style of management was different in every way from her brother's.

So Joe was left out and the Hawks got a couple of bad breaks. Hanif took a knock early on and was never very effective after that; the referee disallowed what appeared to be a perfectly good goal by Callum and they only just clung on for a 0–0 draw that was disappointing in every way. The match after that was against the League leaders, Fordun Rovers, and the Hawks suffered their second defeat since Lynda became coach. Fordun, she'd already discovered, were easily the best team around and she'd devised a stronger defensive formation to cope with their mobile, skilful forwards, drafting a new player, Matthew Longcroft, into the back four. Matthew, a recent arrival in Hurlford after a family move from Yorkshire, was a strong kicker and particularly good in the air. Even his solid contribution, however, wasn't enough to keep the versatile Fordun forwards at bay. Hawks kept them down to a single goal at half-time but in the final quarter-of-an-hour of the match they simply over-ran the despairing defence and scored thrice more.

It really was a comprehensive defeat for the Hawks and Lynda was taken aback to see how drained the players looked as they trudged from the pitch. She wouldn't have guessed how much damage it would do to them mentally after a run of success. Somehow, she had to find a way of boosting their morale before the next fixture.

Then came the crisis.

9

Playing the Pinchers

HANIF WAS STUDYING A BOOK ON soccer tactics by a former Arsenal manager when Lynda telephoned him on the Friday evening. Because his parents were out he answered the phone and her inquiry about his ankle which was still not better from the injury during the Reskington Raiders match.

'Er, it's improving, I hope,' he said carefully, remembering what his mother had told him about taking care of his body ('It's the only one you have, my son, so you must always cherish it').

'So you'll be able to play on Sunday, then? We'll definitely need you, Hanif!'

'I hope so,' he said again, knowing his chances were slim. 'But the hospital, when we went there for the X-ray, said there was no break but a lot of bad bruising. It must not be put under stress, my ankle.'

'Right, well rest as much as you can until Sunday morning, Hanif,' she advised. 'At your age I'm sure you'll recover very quickly. Don't suppose you've got a friend who's free to play for us, have you? Someone who's not appeared in this League yet?'

'Sorry, no,' he replied, like everyone else she'd asked so far. Before taking over the Hawks she'd never have believed there was such a shortage of boys available to play for a Sunday League side.

To her relief, it was Alan Roimond himself, rather than his father, who answered when Lynda telephoned. 'Am I interrupting anything?' she inquired courteously.

'Er, no, not really. I was just trying to invent a new tyre lever. For repairing bikes quicker, you know.'

'Oh, I'm impressed,' she told him, and she was. She hadn't known anything about his off-pitch interests. 'Well, Alan, I'd be grateful if you could invent some players for the Hawks. We may need one or two on Sunday. Any ideas, anyone you know?'

He thought hard but couldn't provide a single name, real or imaginary. He felt he ought to tell her that he might not be free to play either. He was torn between the Hawks and visiting a garage his dad was thinking of buying into as a partner. It would be full of fascinating, sophisticated engineering equipment he might get a chance to try out. But he didn't want to worry her, so he said nothing.

Red Herring wasn't available to talk to Lynda because, his mother reported, he was out helping his dad with the weekly shopping. 'Always together, those two, you know. Carl's a real man's boy,' Mrs Herring said, with a hint of tortured pride. The thing that surprised Lynda was that Red's real name was Carl. Nobody had ever called him that in her hearing.

Lynda Hesketh's last call, after getting no reply from Ricky Dezille or Aaron Quaintance, was to her captain. Thankfully, he was at home and said he was reading a book and didn't mind being interrupted. She couldn't resist asking him about the book, realising that, in Callum's case, it could be on any subject.

'Oh, it's all about South America,' he revealed. 'That's where I fancy going if I get picked for an England tour. Sounds a terrific place, and I don't think some of the countries are all that bothered about rules. It says here that "there's a belief in freedom of expression, both socially and artistically and, particularly, in important areas of sporting enthusiasms".'

'Well, yes, seems so,' she agreed, thoroughly impressed by his choice of reading matter. She could visualise his wry grin as he gave her that information and wished they were having this conversation in the same room. For a couple of minutes they discussed team affairs, recent results, prospects and inevitably her worries about the composition of the team for the match against North Pinchbeck, a side popularly known as 'The Pinchers' and not only for the most obvious reason. They had a reputation for snatching victory from the jaws of defeat or escaping with a draw after being outplayed for much of a match.

'Cal, we're going to have problems on Sunday if we don't find at least one more player to turn out for us,' she told him. 'Matthew's gone down with measles – what a time to choose! – and Aaron's parents are taking him to visit relatives in Kings Lynn. I've just rung to try to get them to change their minds but there's no reply. Oh, and I'm worried about Hanif. You know he's got a damaged ankle? Well, it's plainly still bothering him and I rate him doubtful for Sunday. So if *he* is out we're down to eleven players at best. No sub, therefore. And who knows what else might go wrong?'

Callum sympathised and murmured that things'd probably sort themselves out. There was a baseball programme coming up on TV in ten minutes and he wasn't going to miss that for anything. 'I'll play hard enough for *two* players if we're short,' he told her comfortingly.

'You always do,' she responded, and presently rang off, their problems still unresolved.

When they assembled at the tree-bordered North Pinchbeck ground half-an-hour before the kick-off on Sunday morning, she sensed it was going to be a difficult day. The trees were there to offer some protection against the winds that regularly whistled bone-piercingly across the flat lands from the North Sea; but today rain was combining with a wintry blast to make her thankful *she* wasn't having to play in only a shirt and shorts. The referee, when he turned up, gave her a look of deep suspicion when she greeted him as cheerfully as possible. And she'd already been overtaken, on the winding road to the ground, by a car bearing the ominous '13' on its number-plate.

Ricky, to whom she'd given a lift becuse his bike had been stolen, started shivering within moments of getting out of the car. 'Wish I'd brought another sweater,' he remarked plaintively, adding hopefully: 'D'you think the ref might call it off?'

She shook her head and started counting the Hawks as they arrived, one by one, mostly on bikes, some dropped off by parents and, finally, Alan, who, heroically, had walked from a fairly distant bus stop, having fallen out with his dad over how they spent the morning. Mr Roimond had insisted on going to the garage at the time the match was on, whereas Alan had thought they could have managed both outings with better planning. His dad had gone off in a huff by himself.

'Where's Joe?' she asked but they all shook their heads. 'Did he say he wasn't coming?' Apparently not. Aaron, too, was missing, along with the stricken Matthew, and the Hawks managed to reach full-strength only because Callum had persuaded a younger boy, Peter Greetland, to turn out for them. He looked, to Lynda, too frail to be playing for anyone, let alone in this vicious wind, but Callum said: 'He's tougher than he looks and he can kick like a mule. I know, he once caught me on the shin when a bunch of us were just having a kick-about. He can be dynamite.'

Lynda hoped so and said how grateful she was for a new player. All the same, she felt in her bones that the Hawks would be grounded by these opponents. In their all-white strip, coloured only by a pale green band across the chest, North Pinchbeck were supposed to appear angelic. Their manner suggested otherwise. Most of them seemed to have narrow faces with half-closed eyes (actually the result of so often trying to avoid the freezing winds that crossed the unresisting plain) which gave them an air of sinister purposefulness. One boy was an exception to the general shape, his body as round as his face; but he had splendid ball control and the Pinchers' play literally seemed to revolve round him.

'Whatever else you do, don't get injured,' their coach pleaded with the Hawks before they went on to the pitch. She checked with Hanif, who was walking very tenderly on his right foot, but he insisted he was all right. He was far from certain he'd be able to last out a game but he wasn't going to let Lynda down by crying off.

Peter Greetland was in action as stand-in left-back immediately, darting across to intercept a long pass, bringing the ball swiftly under control and then finding Callum with a well-judged pass of his own. Lynda nodded approvingly. Perhaps her fears were exaggerated after all. Five minutes later she had proof they were not. Pinchbeck, with the wind at their backs, launched a powerful raid down their right flank with skilful exchanges of passes between three players. Peter, sliding in successfully for a tackle, emerged with the ball only to have his heels clipped by an opponent. When he stumbled the ball was whipped away from him by another adversary who took the opportunity to kick Peter on the knee while shielded from sight of the referee.

Incensed, Peter chased after him and brought the thin-faced boy crashing to the ground with the force of an earth-mover. Naturally, the ref spotted it and his hand was reaching for his notebook and card even before he summoned the culprit to stand before him. While the Pinchbeck coach dashed to attend to the writhing victim, Peter was given the fiercest mauling by the ref who then, to the astonishment of all the Hawks and the delight of the Pinchers, flourished his red card.

'But – but – I haven't been booked before. I mean, why not the yellow card?' Peter protested.

'Violent conduct, of which you were all too plainly guilty, receives the severest punishment, young man,' was the answer. 'You may well have put your opponent out of this game. The least you deserve is to be expelled. Now, leave the pitch at once.'

Lynda thought about trying to intervene on Peter's behalf as he trudged disconsolately towards her, but she concluded the ref wasn't likely to be influenced by news that the offender had been playing for the Hawks for less than ten minutes and (she hoped) had no previous record of violence. Refs didn't give second chances to those they'd just dismissed. But Peter's rush of blood had left his team in a parlous position.

Worse was to follow. Before Callum had really had a chance to re-organise the defence, the Hawks were a goal down. Pinchbeck's roly-poly playmaker provided the precise pass that sent a winger on his way at a speed that surprised Davey Ramsden. When the ball was played back into the middle, no one was marking Pinchbeck's two-footed striker and he lobbed the ball into the net as Ricky hesitated before coming off his line. Pinchbeck doubled their score with a crisp header after the ball had been headed-on from a corner kick. It was beginning to look as though it might become a rout.

Lynda tried to communicate instructions to defenders to pick up the danger men, but in the confusion in the Hawks' ranks nothing was being acted on or remembered. Yet they somehow managed to hold out against further relentless attacks until two minutes from half-time. After winning another corner which led to a goal-mouth scramble, Pinchbeck forced the ball into the net after it had rebounded from a post and struck the diving Ricky on the back of the head, leaving him so dizzy he didn't know what was going on. Alan Roimond immediately claimed that their striker had actually punched the ball as he threw himself forward to make contact. The ref, unsighted at the crucial moment, ignored all protests and signalled a goal. It was only when he'd returned to the middle that his attention was drawn by Callum to Ricky's suffering.

By then Lynda was racing across the pitch to attend to the stricken goalkeeper. 'I feel muzzy,' he told her. 'They didn't score, did they?'

'Never mind about that,' she told him. 'I'm sending you off to hospital for a check-up.' He protested, but to no avail: she knew he may have suffered concussion and needed professional treatment. The ref, suddenly sympathetic, agreed and promptly persuaded a home supporter to take the boy to hospital in his car, wrapped in picnic rugs from the boot to keep him warm. Lynda was torn between accompanying him and trying to help her team and it was the ref who made up her mind for her. 'He'll be in good hands with Jeff and you can pick him up when the game's over.'

Callum declared that it was his job to keep goal now and Lynda nodded. There was no alternative because no one else wanted the job and the Hawks were down to nine players. 'I'd've sent you off myself if the ref hadn't,' she heard Callum mutter to Peter at half-time. 'You must've been mad to tackle like that.' Glumly Peter nodded. 'I was,' he conceded. Lynda, even in the midst of so many problems, congratulated herself on her choice of captain. She couldn't imagine any other player who'd have the characater to send off a team-mate at the beginning of the match: or, indeed, at any stage. What's more, Peter was his school-mate and, although younger, a close friend of Callum's.

The second-half, when rain arrived to support the dying wind, was no better than the first for the Hawks: but at least it was no worse. They let in another three goals but Callum's acrobatics and some slices of luck prevented more. The Pinchers were thrilled with a 6–0 victory. After all, they usually just scraped home by the odd goal.

Hurlford looked exhausted when the final whistle sounded and Lynda wished she could do something practical to lift their spirits. Instead, she had to leave them to their showers, which at least were hot, while she hurried away to see how Ricky was getting on at hospital.

'See you tomorrow for training,' she told Callum. 'We'll sort things out then. We'll really plan our future.'

'We'd better,' Callum said. 'Otherwise I think some of the boys'll pack it in. A six-nil thumping takes some getting over.'

Lynda nodded. 'Agreed. But don't dwell on it. You *all* showed lots of character out there in spite of the result. You never gave in, not one of you. *That* is what we're going to build on.'

10

*On the
way up*

JOE KELLY WAS CHOPPING SAVAGELY AT a large, prickly bush when Callum and Hanif eventually tracked him down. His mother had explained he was earning extra pocket money by gardening for a neighbour. They watched, unobserved, for a few moments before announcing their presence. He didn't express any surprise at their visit.

'What d'you want?' he asked, still swinging his arm-long cutters to get into the heart of the bush.

'We need you back in the Hawks' defence,' Callum said in his customary direct manner. 'We had a bad result against Pinchbeck and lost again last week against Garwood. I know you're not playing for anyone else so you ought to come back to us.'

'Has Lynda sent you?' Joe wanted to know, pausing at last.

Callum shook his head. 'She doesn't know what we're up to. But we want the Hawks to get to the top. We've had bad luck but we can go places. Lynda says so and I believe her.'

'So do I,' Hanif put in.

'She didn't want me, she didn't want me as skipper or anything else,' Joe pointed out. 'So what's the point?'

'The Hawks really mean a lot to you, that's the point,' Callum explained carefully. 'When you're on form you're good at chopping opponents down, better than when you chop trees down! You don't do so much damage against players.'

Joe managed to look pleased at that compliment. His pride wouldn't have allowed him to return to the Hawks without an invitation, but he missed playing and being with the rest of the boys more than he could have imagined when he'd walked out on the team.

'Why did she make *you* captain?' he couldn't resist asking. 'I mean, you gave up on a game once and another time you said you were injured when you weren't. How does that make you a leader?'

Callum shrugged. 'It's what Lynda wanted and I've gone along with it.' His pause was only momentary before he added: 'Anyway, you can have the captaincy back, if it means so much to you.'

Hanif was horrified to hear that offer; if accepted, his own position would be meaningless. He gave Callum a sharp look but somehow kept silent until Joe responded.

'Don't suppose it matters that much,' the former skipper said, to his own as well as to the others' surprise. 'But I want a promise I'll not be dropped again, unless I'm injured or something like that. I want her, Lynda, to make a solemn promise.'

'Fine!' exclaimed Callum cheerfully, mission accomplished. 'Come and tell her that yourself. We're having a celebration meal together, all of us, at Pietro's Pizza Place tomorrow. Six o'clock.'

Joe blinked with astonishment. 'But what're you celebrating? I mean, you've just said, the Hawks have been losing every week.'

Hanif, nodding, eyes alight, rushed to answer. 'Yes, but Lynda says we need a pick-up, so she wants to give us a treat. She says it will be good for us all to be together for a meal. It will give us a sense of – sense of –'

'– *camaraderie*,' supplied Callum. 'Means, sort of togetherness, all for one, one for all, everybody for Hurlford!'

'It'll be great, Joe, I *know* it will,' Hanif insisted. 'So come with us.'

'Okay,' Joe replied. 'Might as well, I suppose.'

Pietro himself took their orders. Sporting a tall, white chef's hat, he beamed at everyone in turn in the true manner of the Italian restaurant owner for whom serving good food is the happiest way of making a living.

'Go on, choose what you like,' Lynda Hesketh urged as Red Herring hesitated, his eyes flickering from the top of the long menu card to the bottom and back again. 'They are all good. I eat here often and I've tried most dishes.'

Pietro's beam was of an even higher wattage as he acknowledged her support of his establishment. 'What're anchovies – is that how you say it?' Red inquired, his interest now anchored over a *pizza Napoletana*.

'Small, quite salty fish with a sharp taste. Delicious, Red, I assure you,' she told him.

Callum laughed. 'With a name like yours you ought to eat 'em all the time,' he told Red, who'd long given up worrying about jokes on his name.

'Not at all, that would be cannibalism!' Hanif exclaimed, which made everyone laugh, including Red.

'Right, that's what I'm going to have,' Red declared defiantly, earning a 'Good for you' comment from Lynda and the promise from Pietro that the anchovies would be replaced by something else immediately if Red didn't like them.

After all the orders had been noted down, and glasses of Coke were being rapidly emptied, the talk was all about football and the Hawks' future prospects. As Lynda had hoped, the atmosphere became so relaxed that the boys felt they could discuss anything to do with their own skills or shortcomings, their fears and ambitions for themselves as well as for the team. For a good part of the time she simply listened, merely encouraging the airing of a particular topic now and again with a comment or question.

She saw how they tended to defer a little to Callum, who so obviously had earned their respect as captain; but they also listened to Joe. It was plain to her they'd accept him back into the fold, having understood his reasons for staying away for a couple of matches. Callum's spell in goal had impressed them enormously, not least because no one else had fancied the job, and Ricky, who'd made a swift recovery from his knock on the head, was badgering him to take over between the posts permanently so that he could play as a winger.

In spite of being the youngest present by at least a

year, Peter Greetland had plenty to say for himself. He'd apologised to everyone for letting the team down by getting himself sent off against Pinchbeck but now, having served his one-match suspension under Kellington League rules, he was available for selection again. In training he'd proved to be as energetic as Hanif and tough enough to take the hardest knocks without complaint, in spite of his fragile appearance. Lynda had the feeling that in future he and Callum would form a formidable partnership in the team, so long as Callum could keep a rein on Peter's explosive temper. But then, she had been given plenty of evidence of her captain's control of events on the pitch. She knew without any shadow of a doubt that she'd made the perfect choice in Callum Douglas Collins for he, more than anyone, herself included, had created the sort of team spirit that would carry Hurlford far along the road to success.

'Well,' she said at last, when everyone looked as though they couldn't eat another crumb, 'I suppose we'd better let Signor Pietro have his tables back. Those people in the queue are beginning to look daggers at us!'

There was a chorus of 'Thank you's!' and a 'terrific food!' from Alan, who'd probably eaten more than anyone. Joe, who'd been wondering how to put his question all evening, hurriedly asked: 'Do you make pizzas like these at home, Mrs Hesketh?'

'No,' she answered, mildly surprised.

'Oh, doesn't Marcus like pizzas? I mean, I thought you might have brought him with you tonight.'

She had a glimmer of what Joe was getting at. 'No, I wouldn't have done that,' she answered. 'This is a Hawks team meeting. Nobody else would've been allowed to join us.'

'But Marcus –' Joe persisted.

'Look, I'd better be frank with you,' she said. 'Marcus doesn't live with me. He lives with his father. That's why I don't make him pizzas at home, though I do take him out for them when I can, Joe. I can guess what's worrying you and the answer is that Marcus isn't available to join the Hawks, so he won't be taking your place in the team. Okay?'

'Oh yes, Mrs Hesketh, thanks. Oh, I mean, I'm sorry –' he floundered.

'That's all right, don't say any more, Joe,' she said, her smile returning. 'These things happen all the time.'

'You can say that again,' Alan murmured, but so quietly no one noticed.

'Anyway,' she concluded, 'I want to thank you all for coming. It's been a great evening for me, too, and I have no doubt we're all in just the right mood to show Wispington Red Stars that we're on our way to the top of the table! See you all Sunday.'

'Oh, we'll shoot those Stars down, no danger!' Callum cracked, and they all left Pietro's Pizza Place on a wave of laughter.

Although in a mid-table position, Wispington Red Stars began like high-flyers, as every team seemed to do against the Hawks, Lynda reflected. Red Star's coach, who hadn't even deigned to speak to her before the match, urged his team on with frantic cries of 'Get at 'em, get at 'em' and 'stop bunching – spread out, lads!' Lynda wondered which he would lose first, his voice or his team's attention. She thought it might be a dead-heat.

With Joe restored to the team, the Hawks had a new back-four and in those opening minutes they looked distinctly unsure of themselves. Lynda had told them time and again to talk to each other at critical times: 'Yell when it's your ball and you're going for it; and yell when you can warn somebody to watch out! Players are just like everyone else, they haven't eyes in the back of their heads.' She wished they'd remembered that when Joe and Peter both hesitated over a fifty-fifty ball with Wispington's striker. He kept going, reached the ball first, knocked it sideways to his partner – and his partner hit a first-time shot into the roof of the net before Ricky could move to close him down.

Red Star's coach was predictably ecstatic: 'That'll show 'em, that'll show 'em. Get at 'em again, Star!' He cast a triumphant glance at Lynda. She ignored it.

The star was prominently displayed on the chest of the green shirts that Wispington favoured to go with red shorts; and it was soon shining in Hurlford's penalty area again. This time it was Davey Ramsden who was at fault during an attack, upending his opponent practically on the line separating the penalty area from the rest of the pitch. After a hard look at the relevant spot the ref awarded a free kick – and Lynda breathed a sigh of relief that it wasn't a penalty. There could only have been millimetres in it, she suspected.

She saw Callum having a quiet word with Peter and Joe and guessed he was telling them to forget about their earlier mistake and to concentrate on keeping the enemy out this time. He'd already spoken to Davey as he moved back into the box to aid his defence. He'd vowed he would take the captaincy seriously and he was proving as good as his word.

Wispington's coach dashed along the touchline, screaming at his team to take the kick in the way he'd told them to – and got a warning glance from the ref, a young woman with short, auburn hair. Lynda hoped she'd have the courage to warn him about his conduct if he kept on with his illegal coaching. Happily, the kick came to nothing. Callum rose to head the ball away and Ricky promptly completed the clearance.

On the rain-slicked surface, keeping possession wasn't easy and twice in rapid succession Hanif let slip good chances to make progress when failing to control passes. Lynda wondered whether he'd really recovered from his recent ankle injury; he was the type who'd play on however much he was handicapped by pain or muscle problems. It was too soon to think of replacing him but it was in her mind that Peter Greetland could be moved to a central role while Matthew Longcroft, a substitute today, could be slotted into the back-four very comfortably.

Then Aaron, improving with every match, burst out of midfield, holding on to the ball with fierce determination. 'Get 'im, get 'im!' the Red Star coach roared; but his defence couldn't cope with a player of Aaron's strength and willingness to battle in every situation. Callum, running diagonally off the ball, completely flummoxed his marker by changing wings. Then, as Alan Roimond moved sharply into the middle, there was no one on hand to collar Callum as he picked up Aaron's clever back-heel. The spare defender had decided to challenge Alan the moment Hurlford's midfielder got the ball – and so the way was clear for Callum to sprint ahead. All the time, though, as he drew other defenders towards him, Callum was waiting for the moment to release the ball into Alan's path, a move rehearsed innumerable times in the week's intensive training.

Alan's pace took opponents completely by surprise: and, in any case, they were sure he'd pass to Aaron, now veering away sharply to his left in what was a planned decoy movement.

Without reducing his speed at all, Alan controlled the ball, jinked to go left, turned to the right and, in the same flowing movement, hit it with all his strength. Barely rising a centimetre above the grass, the ball fizzed unerringly into the bottom right-hand corner of the net, way beyond the mesmerised keeper. It was his first goal for Hurlford that season and it couldn't have thrilled him more. Callum, the clever provider, was the first to congratulate him before the rest of the team mobbed him. Wispington's coach, like many of his team, looked numb with shock: nobody had ever told them that the Hawks could display such speed and incisiveness in attack. His hopes of an easy victory were melting away.

On the other hand, Hurlford weren't able to score again before half-time, hard as they tried. Twice they were thwarted by the woodwork, twice by lucky last-ditch tackles, once by over-ambition on Aaron's part when he rounded the goalkeeper and failed to blast the ball into the net when it would have been easier to steer it home with the side of his foot. It wasn't easy for his team-mates to accept his apology for such a basic error for it happened on the stroke of half-time; so the teams went into the changing-room on level terms instead of with Hurlford leading, as they should have been.

Because she was concerned about Hanif's ankle, Lynda didn't at first realise what was going on between Peter and Joe. Hanif had rolled his sock down and her fingers were probing for signs of further bruising or swelling beneath the skin. He showed no signs of more discomfort and so her mind became more attentive to what she was hearing.

'Honestly, Pete, it was *your* ball, not mine,' Joe was insisting. 'But if you'd called I'd've gone for it. Then we wouldn't have given away a stupid goal.'

'Sorry,' Peter said calmly. 'But it was nearer you than me. Next time I won't wait, that's for sure.'

She didn't say a word to them because she didn't need to; it said so much for the new spirit in the team that, almost half-an-hour after it had happened, two players could still show so much concern about an error in defence. It didn't really matter who was at fault for both recognised they should have reacted better to the situation.

'I think they're a bit weak down their left side,' Callum told her. 'That red-headed lad in the back four can't kick with his left foot and he's not much better with his right! I think we should play on him.'

'Brilliant,' she nodded. 'I must admit I hadn't spotted that but you're right, Cal. We have to exploit any weakness we find in the opposition. Good thinking. We'll have a word with Hanif and Alan about it.'

Fortunately, the Wispington coach was doing too much shouting to do any thinking and was not aware of Hurlford's tactical switch – until it was too late. Although the green-shirted attackers pressed forward the moment the game was resumed, and their mid-fielders surged through to join them, they couldn't make any impression on the Hawks' defence, now looking organised and resourceful. At the earliest opportunity, Davey whacked the ball out to Alan Roimond. After a quick one-two exchange with Aaron, Alan took the ball at pace up the right flank, defenders falling back ahead of him as they waited for him to send over the obvious centre.

But Alan kept going, dribbling, still at speed, and looking certain to reach the dead-ball line. At last the red-haired opponent decided to try a tackle – and promptly fell sideways to the turf as Alan swivelled round him. 'Get up, get up, you stupid idiot!' his coach raged, doing nothing, of course, to help his player's confidence. Sweeping in to the edge of the box, Alan picked out Aaron, coming in from the opposite corner and drove the ball towards him.

Aaron's leap took him above the defence and he headed the ball down and back for Callum to take on the half-volley. And the ball was struck with accuracy and venom, a shot that gave the goalkeeper no earthly chance of making a save.

'What a goal!' Lynda exclaimed. But Matthew didn't hear her because he was madly cheering it, too. In its simplicity and execution, it was a classic. What made it doubly enjoyable to the Hawks was that the approach to it had been thought out and carried through to perfection.

Although the Hawks scored again, five minutes from time when a weary Red Star defender miskicked in front of goal to provide the predatory Aaron with a tap-in, it was the goal that effectively won the match. It was the first time since she'd become their coach that the Hawks had come from behind to win a match. That alone was significant to Lynda. Team spirit and determination were now allied to resilience.

When the final whistle shrilled, Peter celebrated in style by performing a series of cartwheels across the middle of the pitch. Joe, his face lighting up like a beacon with the thrill of the victory, surprised himself as well as everyone else by doing a kind of tribal dance on the spot. The rest of the players flung their arms around each other and then waltzed back and forth across the penalty area. Then, in recognition of his brilliance throughout the match, Aaron and Hanif hoisted Callum on to their shoulders for a triumphal circuit of the pitch.

Lynda, wondering how on earth they still had energy for such high jinks, stood and applauded them until, at last, they calmed down and headed for the dressing-room. There she shook each of them by the hand and, with Callum, shared a warm embrace.

'Keep playing like that, boys, and we'll go to the top,' she told them as they sank down on to the benches. 'You were really great today.'

'We're going to be the *greatest* Sunday League team you ever saw,' responded Callum euphorically. 'Right, lads, right?'

'Right!' his team yelled in unison.